A NOTE TO PARENTS

When your children are ready to "step into reading," giving them the right books is as crucial as giving them the right food to eat. **Step into Reading Books** present exciting stories and information reinforced with lively, colorful illustrations that make learning to read fun, satisfying, and worthwhile. They are priced so that acquiring an entire library of them is affordable. And they are beginning readers with a difference—they're written on five levels.

Early Step into Reading Books are designed for brand-new readers, with large type and only one or two lines of very simple text per page. **Step 1 Books** feature the same easy-to-read type as the Early Step into Reading Books, but with more words per page. **Step 2 Books** are both longer and slightly more difficult, while **Step 3 Books** introduce readers to paragraphs and fully developed plot lines. **Step 4 Books** offer exciting nonfiction for the increasingly independent reader.

The grade levels assigned to the five steps—preschool through kindergarten for the Early Books, preschool through grade 1 for Step 1, grades 1 through 3 for Step 2, grades 2 through 3 for Step 3, and grades 2 through 4 for Step 4—are intended only as guides. Some children move through all five steps very rapidly; others climb the steps over a period of several years. Either way, these books will help your child "step into reading" in style!

To Uncle Billy Estay:
Where are you?
Call Bobby!
— C. M.

Photographs: Pages 14, 20, 27, 45, Corbis/Bettmann; page 15, Science
Museum/Science & Society Picture Library; page 18, Steinbrugge Collection,
Earthquake Engineering Research Center, University of California, Berkeley.

Special thanks to Dr. Waverly Person, Chief of the National Earthquake
Information Service, U.S. Geological Survey, for his help with this book.

Library of Congress Cataloging-in-Publication Data
McMorrow, Catherine.
Quakes! / by Catherine McMorrow ; illustrated by Stephen Marchesi.
p. cm. — (Step into reading. A step 4 book)
SUMMARY: Examines earthquakes, what causes them and their results, and looks
at some notable earthquakes.
ISBN 0-679-86945-X (trade) — ISBN 0-679-96945-4 (lib. bdg.)
1. Earthquakes—Juvenile literature. [1. Earthquakes.] I. Marchesi, Stephen, ill.
II. Title. III. Step into reading. Step 4 book.
QE521.3.M394 2000 551.22—dc21 99-049400

www.randomhouse.com/kids

Printed in the United States of America November 2000 10 9 8 7 6 5 4 3 2 1

Step into Reading®

QUAKES!

By Catherine McMorrow
Illustrated by Stephen Marchesi

A Step 4 Book

Random House 🏠 New York

Chapter 1

January 17, 1994
Northridge, California
Magnitude: 6.7

It was just before dawn.

Bill Estay was home in his third-floor apartment, taking a shower. The bar of soap squirted out of his hand and plopped into the tub. Bill reached down to pick it up.

Suddenly, the tub started swinging back and forth like a rowboat in a storm! Bill grabbed onto the shower curtain, but it tore. He was thrown sideways out the bathroom door and landed on his piano in the living room. He could hear dishes crashing in the kitchen. Pictures fell off the wall. Books shot out of the bookcase. *"Dear God in heaven,"* Bill thought. *"It's an earthquake!"*

Then the floor began to tilt. Everything in the room went sliding toward the front wall.

Bill jumped off the piano and scrambled back up to the bathroom. He grabbed hold of the door frame. All his furniture was now piled under the living room window.

Suddenly, there was a loud ripping sound. Plaster dropped from the ceiling. The windows shattered. Bill could not believe his eyes. The entire front wall fell off the building, and his furniture thundered into the parking lot below!

A cloud of plaster dust made Bill cough and gag. His eyes stung. His heart thumped madly.

After a few minutes, the air cleared. In the dim light, Bill could see his whole neighborhood. It looked like a giant toy box dumped on its side. Hundreds of car alarms were going off. Then came the wail of sirens and the *thup-thup-thup* of helicopters circling overhead.

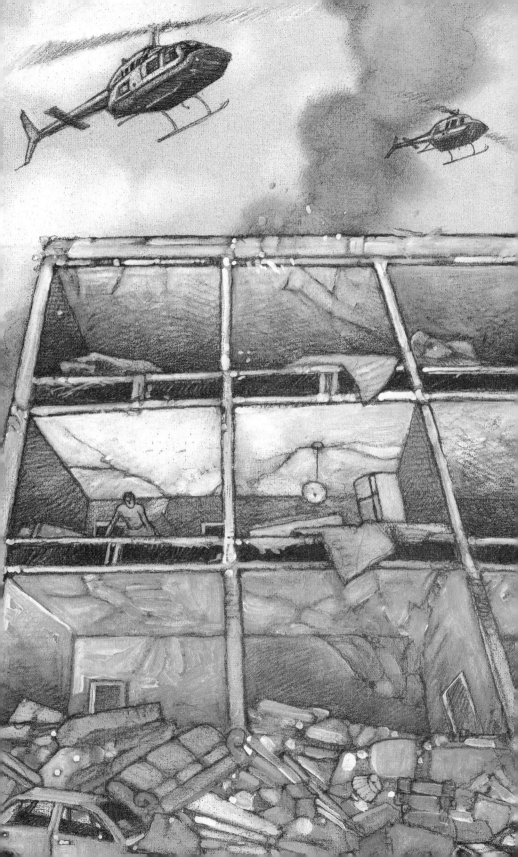

Bill wrapped himself in the shower curtain and crawled out the bathroom window. Carefully, he made his way down the bent and wobbly fire escape. From every direction, people were calling for help. A man handed a little girl to Bill through a window. Bill carried her across the street to a group of women who had spread blankets on the ground. He helped other children find their parents.

In all the commotion, no one noticed that Bill was wearing two left shoes and a shower curtain!

When the sun came up, Bill found a pair of pants hanging on a parking meter. He was very grateful that they fit.

The entire area of Northridge was a disaster area. Water from broken pipes gushed through the streets. Gas pipes exploded and shot fireballs into the air. Palm trees went up in flames, like great torches.

Rescue teams searched the wrecked buildings for survivors. They used specially trained dogs to sniff out people who were buried alive in the rubble. They found one man whose ceiling had collapsed on top of him. He was trapped against the floor with only eight inches of breathing space. Rescuers cheered him on for an hour as he wiggled to a place where they could pull him out.

Hospitals all over Los Angeles turned their parking lots into outdoor emergency rooms. One nurse used an orange traffic cone as a megaphone, yelling instructions to the crowd. A man had a heart attack, while nearby, a baby was born. Doctors and nurses treated hundreds of people for cuts and burns. They did everything they could, but not everyone was saved.

Seismologists (size-MOL-uh-jists)—scientists who study and predict earthquakes—were surprised by the Northridge quake. It began in a hidden *fault,* or crack, deep in the earth.

Some nine miles below Bill Estay's apartment—just as he dropped his bar of soap—an explosion went off with the force of an atom bomb. Shock waves traveling 10,000 miles per hour zigzagged in every direction. They rocketed to the earth's surface and burst through the ground, shaking and tearing everything in their path.

Scientists sometimes explain a quake this way: Think of the earth as a chocolate-covered cherry. The cherry is the *core,* or center, of the earth. The gooey liquid around the core is superheated liquid rock. The chocolate shell is the earth's *crust*—the ground we walk on. Now imagine that the chocolate shell is cracked in pieces. This is

what the earth's surface is like. It is made up
of giant pieces of the crust, called *plates,*
floating on the molten rock.

   These plates are always moving, though
very slowly. One may move north, the other
south. Every now and then, they crash and
grind against each other, which causes the
earth to tremble, or "quake."

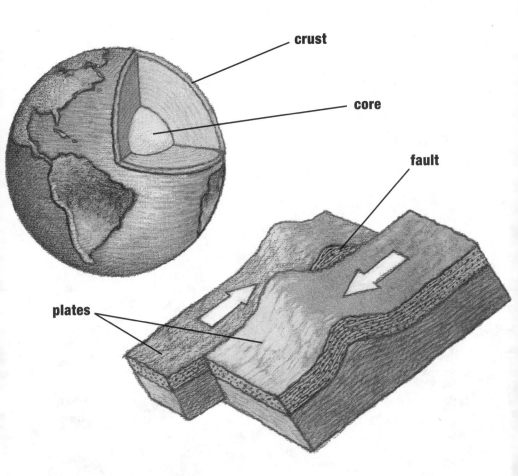

The state of California rests on two pieces of the earth's crust. The place where they come together is an 800-mile-long crack in the earth called the San Andreas Fault.

Some faults, like the San Andreas, are easy to see. But many others are hidden deep beneath the earth's surface. Seismologists monitor these invisible faults with a network of *seismometers* (size-MAH-muh-terz)—underground machines that record ground motion. Modern seismometers can detect movements as small as a spider walking by!

The first known "earthquake detector" was invented in 132 A.D. by the Chinese astronomer and mathematician Chang Heng. It was a vase-shaped vessel with dragon heads around the top and frogs around the bottom. Each dragon held a bronze ball in its mouth. When the earth trembled—even hundreds of miles away— a pendulum inside the jar would swing, knocking a ball from one of the dragon heads into the open mouth of a frog below. By looking at which frog the ball fell into, the scientists could tell in which direction the earthquake was happening.

Nowadays, the shock waves of a quake are recorded on a seismograph. A scientist named Charles Richter (RICK-ter) invented a rating system, called the *Richter scale,* that measures the *magnitude,* or size, of an earthquake. So far, the largest recorded quake measured 9.5 on the Richter scale. There are millions of quakes each year, but most of them are too small for us to feel or record.

The Northridge quake shook for twenty seconds. It registered 6.7 on the Richter scale. Fifty-seven people died and 20,000 were left homeless.

California engineers learned about some mistakes they made in the safety features of their buildings. Still, these modern buildings were much stronger than the buildings were in the San Francisco quake almost ninety years earlier.

Chapter 2

April 18, 1906
San Francisco, California
Magnitude: 7.7–7.9

A low rumbling sound could be heard in the distance. It was quiet at first, but within a few minutes it grew to a roar.

The ground along the waterfront began waving like a magic carpet. Cobblestones in the street popped and jiggled.

People ran from their shaking houses—women in nightgowns, men in underwear and top hats. The streets were filled with broken glass, and nearly everyone was barefooted.

Much of the city had been built on landfill, which is swampy ground that's been filled in with trash. The quake churned the ground into mush.

Whole houses slid down hills. Buildings sank until their second floors were level with the street. Some buildings leaned over so slowly that people could walk down the side and jump to the ground.

But many tall buildings whipped back
and forth. Steel beams screeched as they
ripped apart. Bricks thundered to the
ground. Wounded horses let out strange
cries. Men fell to their knees, shouting, "It's
the end of the world!"

The earth heaved and twisted for a few
horrifying minutes. Then it suffered one last
awful jolt and fell silent.

This fateful day became famous not only for the massive earthquake but for a great fire that happened as a result of the quake. The people of San Francisco were eager to find comfort after such a shock. One lady who still had a home lit her stove to fry some ham and eggs. But her chimney was damaged by the earthquake and it caused a fire.

Similar fires started all over town. Soon the entire city was ablaze with flames 200 feet high in every direction.

People poured into the streets. They pushed sofas stacked with bedding, baby carriages, pianos, and sewing machines. They dodged live electric wires and panicky horses. Horse-drawn ambulances raced wildly back and forth, carrying the injured to medical help.

The city's water pipes had been torn apart by the quake. Firemen had to use water from horse troughs, wine from wine cellars, and even sewage to fight the blaze.

Everywhere the firemen turned, it seemed the flames were headed toward them. They ripped doors from buildings to use as shields against the heat. The heat was so intense that water thrown at the fire turned to steam before it reached the flames! Papers lying in the streets burst spontaneously into flames. Deep inside fireproof bank vaults, silver dollars melted into a precious goo!

Wind whipped the fire into a giant flaming tornado, sending heat waves out over the bay. Boats in the water began to smolder—the paint on their hulls blistered and peeled.

Firemen worked until they dropped from exhaustion and had to be rolled out of harm's way. Most of the city burned to the ground.

Although the quake lasted only a few minutes, the people of San Francisco lost nearly everything from the series of disasters. But they had not lost their courage or their positive attitude. They began to rebuild immediately.

They put up signs with such advice as DON'T TALK FIRE, TALK BUSINESS. One sign that hung in a gutted building read: ONLY TEMPORARILY CLOSED DUE TO ELEVATOR NOT WORKING.

They rebuilt their town bigger and fancier than ever. It was one of many "earthquake recoveries" that San Francisco would face.

There would be more quakes in the future for this earthquake-prone region. But California isn't the only place in the world where big quakes hit. Japan also lies on a fault line—this one under the ocean.

Chapter 3

September 1, 1923
Tokyo, Japan
Magnitude: 8.3

American architect Frank Lloyd Wright had designed a beautiful hotel in Tokyo for the emperor. It had terraces, gardens, and hand-carved stonework. And it was loudly proclaimed to be "earthquake-proof."

On this particular day, 200 guests gathered for the hotel's grand opening. An elegant luncheon was to be served at noon.

But at 11:58, the earth served up its own surprising dish. Three tremendous shocks ripped into the coastline of Japan, shaking the city of Tokyo and the surrounding Kanto Plain.

The ground shuddered for over one minute. When it stopped, the Imperial Hotel had suffered much damage, but was one of the few buildings left standing in the city.

Tokyo's modern business district was destroyed. The tallest building, called the "Rising Over the Clouds Tower," was twelve stories high. During the quake it swayed back and forth, appeared to make a polite bow, and then broke apart. Japanese houses were mostly frail wooden structures with paper windows. They were tossed about like matchboxes.

People all over Tokyo had been preparing their noon meal. Red-hot coals from overturned stoves set the wreckage ablaze.

In rural areas, many people trying to get to safety had to creep on their hands and knees through bamboo groves. The ground had shaken so badly that the bamboo splintered into razor-sharp fragments. Crawling through the groves was deadly. Bamboo fragments can slash a person to ribbons.

At the waterfront, people jumped into the sea to escape the fires. They hoped to be rescued by nearby ships. But the crewmen aboard were fighting their own battles. Flaming pieces of wood and paper had blown from the shore onto the vessels. Many ships caught fire.

To make matters worse, at four o'clock that afternoon, a *cyclone*—a spinning windstorm—crossed over the Kanto Plain. Whirling at 125 miles per hour, it picked up anything in its path—small boats, flaming furniture, and bodies—and hurled it all into the sky. When it dropped everything down again, the flames spread even farther.

Fires burned all night. They cast an eerie light, which a person could read by from ten miles away.

The mayor of Tokyo could hardly believe how much damage the earthquake had done to his city. He hoped to rebuild with safer, squat concrete buildings and wider streets. But within days, the Japanese people were putting up new homes. They built them out of crates, pine boards, and tin. The old flammable city reappeared almost overnight.

Japan has suffered many earthquakes over the years. In fact, the 1995 Kobe quake was smaller—6.9 on the Richter scale—but the devastation was enormous. Over 5,000 people lost their lives, nearly 30,000 were injured, and hundreds of thousands of buildings were destroyed.

No one can say exactly when the next quake will come. In the meantime, Japanese engineers swap ideas with California engineers. They hope to design buildings that will withstand a bigger quake than a 6.9, or even a 7.9—like the one that struck Alaska in 1964.

Chapter 4

March 27, 1964
Anchorage, Alaska
Magnitude: 9.2

In the spring of 1964, Alaska experienced the largest earthquake ever recorded in the United States. Animals seemed to sense something was about to happen. They behaved strangely. Kodiak bears came out of hibernation two weeks early. They left their caves by the sea and shuffled inland. Cows left their pastures and hurried to higher ground. Snakes came out of their holes and lay on the frozen snow.

The shaking began shortly after 5:30 P.M. At first, the earth rocked lightly. In a department store in downtown Anchorage, china dolls quivered on the shelves. Then the whole building began to shake violently. Mirrors and display cases exploded into sparkling shards. Chunks of ceiling came crashing down. The lights went out.

Outside, the street ripped down the middle. One side dropped eleven feet! Parked cars bounced and rammed into each other like bumper cars. The ground began opening in gigantic cracks. People held hands in long chains to keep from falling.

On the edge of town, a real estate agent
was showing a house when the shock waves
struck. "Ignore it," he told his clients as they
stood in the front yard. "We have these
rumblings all the time." But as he spoke, the
entire house tumbled downhill. It broke
apart until it was nothing but a pile of
rubble.

On the coast, fuel tanks exploded. They spewed orange flames and greasy black smoke. Minutes later, a *tsunami* (soo-NAH-mee) hit. "Tsunami" is a Japanese word meaning "harbor wave." It is a huge tidal wave that is created when an earthquake or volcano rocks the ocean floor. The vibration of an underwater quake creates ripples in the water like those formed by tossing a stone into a pond. But these ripples are humongous. They can be 300 feet high—and very fast. Tsunamis can travel up to 600 miles per hour. That's as fast as an F-14 jet fighter plane!

When this wall of water hit, it hurled an entire fleet of fishing boats inland. It knocked a lighthouse off its foundation and tossed cars up into trees. Large docks were smashed to bits. The pieces of wood became coated with fuel oil and caught fire. In the chilly night, they looked like floating candles twinkling all over the bay.

Local pilots flying overhead took photos of the damage. They saw that many people were stranded without food or medical care. The U.S. Army came to the rescue. Soldiers searched for lost loved ones and built temporary shelters. Military cooks served soup and coffee around the clock. They concocted dinners with whatever food they could find in the wrecked buildings and overturned freezers—hot dogs, moose, steak, snake, and bear.

Seismologists from all over came to Alaska. They charted *fissures,* or cracks in the earth, measured cracks in buildings, and noted the direction in which things had fallen. They drilled holes in the ground and set out seismometers. With all their measurements, they calculated that parts of the state had shifted forty-seven feet!

During the next six months, the seismographs recorded 9,200 *aftershocks* in the area. Aftershocks are small tremors that often follow earthquakes. They are similar to the jiggles you would see if you tapped on a piece of gelatin.

Although this was almost the world's largest earthquake, much of the shaking occurred in the wilderness, away from city buildings. Fortunately, the damage was not quite as bad as in the cities of Japan and California. But still, 125 lives were lost, and scientists spent a great deal of time studying the record-breaking quake.

Chapter 5

Since ancient times, people have tried to understand what causes earthquakes. The Algonquin Indians believed that a giant tortoise held the earth on his back, and when he moved, the earth wobbled. Siberians believed there were giant moles tunneling underground, stirring up the dirt and rocks. The people of Mozambique thought the earth sometimes suffered from chills and fever, which made it shiver.

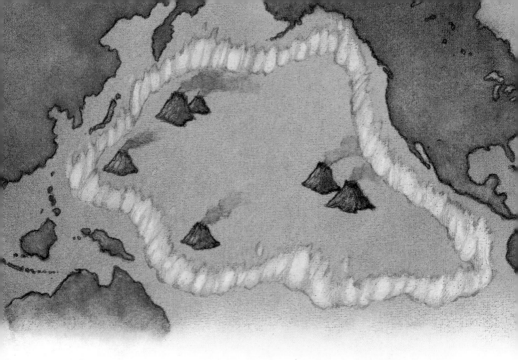

Today we know that most quakes occur in an area around the globe called the Ring of Fire. The Ring of Fire is a pattern of earthquake fault lines that circles the Pacific Ocean. It seems to outline where pieces of the earth's crust bang against each other. The Ring of Fire is also full of hot, bubbling volcanoes.

Scientists monitor the Ring of Fire closely. They watch which pieces of the earth's crust are beginning to move, so they can say where quakes will happen. They just cannot say exactly *when*.

Many seismologists also watch animal behavior, because animals seem to do strange things before a quake. Swans, who live mostly on the water, have run inland to lie down with their feet up before a quake strikes. Leeches and turtles have been known to swim back and forth, rolling over and over.

In China, some people keep catfish to warn them of an upcoming quake. Catfish are normally sluggish bottom dwellers. But hours before a quake, they rise to the surface and become frantic.

Other strange things have been observed right before or during earthquakes. People have seen balls of colored light skipping across the horizon. A bank of red fog has suddenly appeared. Sometimes wine in sealed bottles has turned cloudy, and fresh milk has instantly turned sour!

Once, the crew on a British ship heard hissing sounds coming from the ocean. The water began to bubble and give off a terrible smell. Then hundreds of dead fish floated up to the surface. When the crew raised anchor to leave, they found that the anchor chain was partly melted!

But none of these oddities happen the same way every time there is an earthquake. So scientists keep a close eye on seismographs, and engineers work hard at designing quake-proof buildings.

Engineers test new buildings and bridges by constructing them on top of a giant platform called a *shaking table.* Machines shake the table up, down, and sideways, the way an earthquake would. One shaking table can hold 1,000 tons!

The ancient Mayans and Incas, who lived in the earthquake zones of South America, were good quake engineers. They cut great blocks of stone in many different sizes and shapes, fitting them together with such precision that there was no need for mortar. This type of construction resisted earthquake damage for hundreds of years. It was a good design, but it doesn't work for skyscrapers!

Chapter 6

Even with all our knowledge and technology, earthquakes are just as troublesome today as they were a hundred years ago. Besides being deadly and frightening, they dramatically disrupt everyday life.

After the 1994 Northridge quake, people had to wait in long lines at grocery stores for food. There were lines to use pay phones. Everyone wanted to let their families and friends know that they were okay.

More than 5,000 aftershocks rattled the Los Angeles area and everyone's nerves. Some people were afraid to be in their homes. The slightest noise sent them dashing outside. Others kept hard hats—or even heavy bowls!—close by to protect their heads. They bought steel canopy beds that were supposed to be able to withstand a collapsing roof. Five thousand homeless people stayed in Red Cross shelters. Fifteen thousand camped out in parks, cars, and front yards.

Bill Estay remembered what his mother had always said when he was a child: "Watch the cat—if her fur stands up, a shake is coming!" But Bill didn't have a cat! He did, however, have an earthquake survival kit. He was able to dig it out of the rubble, along with some socks and a bag of low-fat potato chips.

Bill ran into his neighbor Janine in a park across the street from their demolished building. All that she had salvaged from her apartment was a package of licorice and a bottle of Gatorade. They shared their snacks and went through the contents of Bill's survival kit.

Janine took out a jar of Tang, a can of tuna, crackers, a flashlight, and what looked like a small tinfoil pillow. It unfolded into a thin, silvery space blanket. She said, "This is, like, *totally* seismic!"

"Everyone should have an earthquake kit," said Bill. "Now all I need is a cat."

"And," said Janine, "a rubber house that bounces back!"

EARTHQUAKE FACTS

• The largest recorded earthquake—9.5 on the Richter scale—took place May 22, 1960, in Chile, South America. More than 5,000 people died, and 2 million people were left homeless.

• The longer the fault line, the bigger the earthquake and the longer it lasts.

• The states that have the most earthquakes: Alaska and California.

• The states that have the fewest earthquakes: Florida and North Dakota.

• Not all earthquakes cause great loss of life or property damage. How much damage a quake causes depends on how populated an area is, the quality of the buildings, and the ground characteristics (or *site geology*). Large earthquakes often strike remote areas or uninhabited islands in the middle of the ocean, so much less damage is done.